the little
book of

Written and edited by Gill Knappett. The author
has asserted her moral rights.
Designed by Tim Noel-Johnson.
All photographs © Jarrold Publishing except that
on pp 84–85, used by kind permission of Fitzbillies.

Printed in Hong Kong.
ISBN 0-7117-1610-2   1/03

Jarrold Publishing, Healey House, Dene Road, Andover,
Hampshire, SP10 2AA.
Tel: 01264 409200   e-mail: heritagesales@jarrold.com
website: www.britguides.com

Introduction

Cambridge is rich in heritage and history: university buildings of impoverished medieval beginnings jostle with the generous provisions of latter-day benefactors; a magnificent cathedral dominates the skyline; museums and their treasures give fascinating insights into the past; its science-based industry has been at the forefront of the high-tech revolution; and spectacular skies over the surrounding fenland present the most magical of landscapes. Join us in a wealth of over 100 wise, weird, wonderful and wacky facts and anecdotes about this lovely city in this intriguing little book.

First impressions

'When I visited Cambridge, the nakedness of the land was too plainly visible under a sheet of snow, through which gutters and ditches ran, like ink, by the side of leafless sallows, which resembled huge pincushions stuck on posts. The town, however, made amends.'

Leigh Hunt, 1850

Early settlers

Stone Age and Iron Age man were attracted to this marshy fenland with its navigable river and shallow hill. By around AD **400**, the Romans had built a town here surrounded by a wall and had bridged the river at the point where traffic crossed as it journeyed to and from Colchester.

The Granta

The River Cam was once called the Granta, and there is evidence of a bridge existing here from the reference to 'Grantebrycge' in the Anglo-Saxon Chronicle of 875. Upstream, where it flows through the village of Grantchester, the river is still called the Granta.

Conqueror's castle

William the Conqueror built a motte-and-bailey castle on the hill here in 1068, which served as a royal castle and gaol for 200 years. Edward I rebuilt the castle in stone, but during the 15th and 16th centuries the stone was taken to build King's and other colleges, and was finally demolished in 1842. All that remains is the grassy Castle Mound.

Gog Magog ghost

According to legend, if you climb Gog Magog Hills, overlooking Cambridge, on a moonlit night and shout 'Knight. Knight. Tonight come forth!' a phantom knight will appear.

On a clear day ...

Castle Mound is the highest point in Cambridge – Ely Cathedral is visible from the top on a clear day – and it has been said that there is no higher point until the North Pole.

Isle of Ely

Until a draining programme took place in the 17th century, Ely – 24km (15m) north of Cambridge – was known as the Isle of Ely and could only be reached by boat.

City status

Cambridge was granted city status by King George VI in 1951.

TIC tours

Cambridge attracts over 4,000,000 tourists every year. The Tourist Information Centre, situated in The Old Library – a lovely Grade I listed building, offers visitors many guided tours, including visits to colleges, chauffeured punting trips and drama tours to meet, amongst others, Henry VIII, Queen Victoria and Lord Byron.

Cambridgeshire clunch

Many buildings in the city are made of stone or brick combined with 'clunch', a stone-like chalk mined in Cambridgeshire.

One of four

The Round Church – now the centre of Cambridge Christian Heritage – is one of only four surviving round churches in

England. Its design is based on the Church of the Holy Sepulchre in Jerusalem, built in circular form so that pilgrims could walk round the site of the tomb where Jesus rose from the dead.

Ancient church

Historic St Bene't's (Benedict's) Church tower, built c.1025 during King Canute's reign, is the oldest building in the county; parts of the original nave still remain. Circular openings above the belfry windows are thought to have been included in the tower so that owls could enter and catch the church mice.

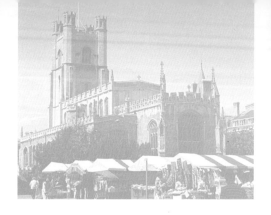

Name that tune

The tune of the chimes of Great St Mary's Church, composed by a university professor, became famous as the Westminster Chimes when they were adopted for Big Ben.

Well worth the climb

Climb the 123 steps to the top of the tower of Great St Mary's for spectacular views across the city and colleges.

Stars and stripes

In Little St Mary's Church is a memorial to Godfrey Washington, one time minister and Fellow of Peterhouse, bearing a coat of arms decorated with stars and stripes. His nephew was George Washington, first president of the USA, and the design on the coat of arms is thought to have been the inspirarion for the American flag.

Animal magic

An extensive range of animal life –
including those now extinct – is displayed
in the Museum of Zoology in preserved,
skeletal or fossilized form.

Kettle's Yard collection

Kettle's Yard was once the home of Jim Ede,
a former curator at the Tate Gallery,
London. The house and contents were
presented to the University of Cambridge
in 1966 and includes Ede's collection of art,
mostly of the first half of the 20th century,
including paintings, sculpture, furniture,
glass, ceramics and natural objects.

Whipple's wonders

The Whipple Museum is home to scientific instruments dating from the Middle Ages and includes such diverse objects as a clockwork model of the solar system (c.1750) and 1980s calculators.

An architect, arts and antiquities

George Basevi, the architect of the neoclassical masterpiece that is the Fitzwilliam Museum and home to Cambridge University's famed art and antiquities collection, fell to his death from the western tower of Ely Cathedral.

Cambridge folk

In the 16th-century building housing the Cambridge and County Folk Museum visitors can discover how people in the area have lived since 1700 – including why the river stank in the 19th century and the mystery of a vanishing policeman.

Great Scott

The Scott Polar Research Institute, founded in 1920, is a memorial to Captain Robert Falcon Scott. The Latin inscription on the front of the building in Lensfield Road translates as 'He sought the secret of the Pole but found the hidden face of God'.

Geological gems

The Sedgwick Museum's collection of geological treasures dates from 3,000 million years ago to the present day and is second only in importance to London's Natural History Museum. One of its local finds from nearby Barrington gravel pit is a 125,000-year-old hippopotamus.

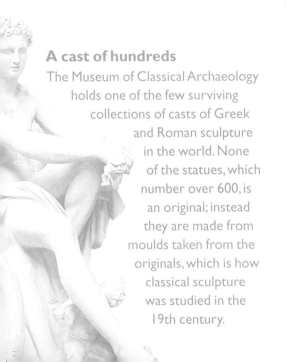

A cast of hundreds

The Museum of Classical Archaeology holds one of the few surviving collections of casts of Greek and Roman sculpture in the world. None of the statues, which number over 600, is an original; instead they are made from moulds taken from the originals, which is how classical sculpture was studied in the 19th century.

Phenomenal phenomenon

'The Cambridge Phenomenon' refers to the rapid and successful growth of science-based industry in and around the city. Cambridge Science Park was England's first science park and is one of the largest in Europe. Established by Trinity College in the 1970s, it attracts multi-national as well as local companies.

Scientific significance

The Cavendish Laboratories have seen numerous scientific achievements. These include Joseph John Thomson's discovery of the electron and, subsequently, his invention of the cathode-ray tube; Ernest Rutherford's discovery of alpha, beta and gamma rays and his prediction of the existence of the neutron; the exploration by John Douglas Cockcroft and Ernest Walton that led to the atom being split; and James Dewey Watson's unravelling of the molecular structure of DNA.

Kingly praise

'I tell you, Sirs, that I judge no land in England better bestowed than that which is given to our Universities. For by their maintenance our Realm shall be well governed when we be dead and rotten.'

Henry VIII

From Oxford to Cambridge

Legend has it that the beginnings of what was to become a great university at Cambridge occurred when in 1209 a group of scholars fled to Cambridge to escape the Oxford riots.

Tripos

A tripos is Cambridge's name for the honours examination leading to a Bachelor of Arts degree. The term dates back to medieval times when exam candidates would dispute a subject with an older graduate sitting on a three-legged stool (a tripos).

Cambridge colleges

Each of Cambridge's 31 colleges, situated in different parts of the city, is an independent institution with its own property and income. Each college  appoints its own staff and selects its own students – approximately one third of applicants are allocated a place. Teaching is shared between the colleges and university departments and degrees are awarded by the university.

Old Schools origin

Until the 16th century most students lived in lodgings and teaching rooms had to be hired; all this changed when the purpose-built complex – now known as the Old Schools – was built.

It's compulsory

Most colleges were founded as theology schools, but in the 18th century mathematics was introduced as the main and compulsory subject of study. The subject ceased to be compulsory 100 years later.

Evening gowns

Until as recently as the 1970s, undergraduates had to wear gowns when out in the city after dark.

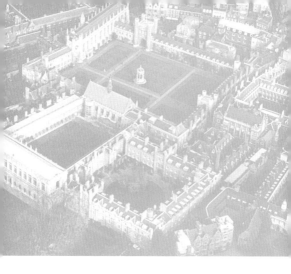

When in Cambridge …

What are called quadrangles in Oxford
are known as courts in Cambridge.

Great Scott

Sir Giles Gilbert Scott designed the University Library, opened in 1934. Its appearance is thought to echo that of the old red telephone boxes, also designed by Scott.

Join our club

Some of the university's more unusual clubs and societies include: Abra-Cam-Dabra Magic Society; Athletic Cartwheeling Society; Cocktail Society; Crazy-Golf Club; Jugglers' Association; Rollerblading Society; Tiddlywinks Club; Ultimate Frisbee Club.

Etonians only

King's College was founded by Henry VI in 1441 for students from his newly established college at Eton. It was only in 1873 that non-Etonians were admitted.

Timeless reminder

After graduating from King's College, Rupert Brooke (1887–1915) lodged in a village nearby and his fond memories of his time at the Old Vicarage, Grantchester, are immortalized in his poem of the same name:

... oh! yet
Stands the church clock at ten-to-three?
And is there honey still for tea?

Quick-drying paint

Rubens' *The Adoration of the Magi*, given to King's College Chapel in 1961, was painted in just eight days in 1634.

Christmas tradition

King's College's world-famous choir has broadcast the Festival of Nine Lessons and Carols from the chapel every Christmas Eve since 1928.

Choir's crocodile

Members of the King's College Choir still walk to and from chapel in crocodile formation, and wear top hats, Eton suits and gowns.

Butts's and Betts's ghosts

The ghost of a Master of Corpus Christi, Dr Henry Butts, is said to haunt the Old Court. Butts hanged himself in despair in 1632 when plague swept the town and the death toll devastated his beloved college. Another ghost, that of a young man named James Betts, haunts the Master's Lodge at Corpus Christi. In 1690 Betts was suffocated after taking refuge in a closet whilst hiding from Dr Spencer, the then Master, who disapproved of Betts's assignations with his daughter, Elizabeth.

Secret burial

Oliver Cromwell, born in nearby Huntingdon, was an undergraduate at Sidney Sussex College. A plaque in the college ante-chapel marks the grave where his head was secretly buried in 1960.

Mathematical Bridge

The wooden bridge popularly known as the Mathematical Bridge at Queens' College is a copy of the 1749 original. It was believed to be built on geometric principles without the aid of nails but there are, in fact, nuts and bolts at its joints.

What time is it?

The unusual sundial at Queens' College is also a moondial. The table of figures beneath the dial is needed to calculate the time.

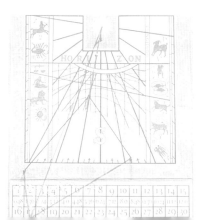

Lawyers' college

Trinity Hall was founded in 1350 to educate men in canon law to replace the 700 parish priests who died of the Black Death. The college specialized in law until the 19th century and is still referred to as the lawyers' college.

Pass the port

In the parlour of Trinity Hall is a half-moon table where Fellows sit to drink port. A remarkable contraption consisting of a small railway with two trucks, operated by a wooden lever, allows the port to circle the table from right to left in traditional manner.

Bridge of Sighs

Two parts of St John's College are linked by the Bridge of Sighs, named after its famous Venetian counterpart.

Oak-apple Day

St John's College still celebrates the restoration of the monarchy on Oak-apple Day (29 May) with a feast and oak boughs decorating the hall.

Curious creatures

On the Great Gate of St John's College, two mythical beasts called yales support the coat of arms of the college's founder. The yales have elephants' tails, antelopes' bodies, goats' heads and horns that turn independently.

Poor phantom

The spectre of James Wood, a past undergraduate and Master of St John's College, has been known to block the narrow staircase in Second Court, only moving out of the way when spoken to. Wood was such an impoverished student that he would sit on the well-lit stairway to save lighting and heating his own room.

Shorthand notebook

Samuel Pepys's diary is housed in the library named after him at Magdalene (pronounced 'maudlin') College, where he was a student. It took three years for the shorthand he used to write the diary to be deciphered.

Magdalene in mourning

In 1988 Magdalene became the last college to admit women students. Male students marked the occasion by wearing black armbands and parading a coffin, with the college flag lowered to half mast.

Spoilsport

One of the statutes of Monks' Hostel (a forerunner of Magdalene College) was that 'students of this College are to visit taverns less often than other students'.

Long-running tradition

The clock on Trinity College's Great Court has a double strike of a low and high note. Undergraduates are challenged to run around the court while the clock strikes twelve, a tradition featured in the film *Chariots of Fire*.

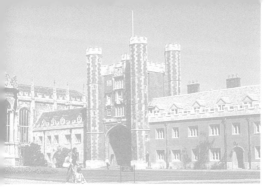

Student prank

As a result of a student prank in the 19th century, the statue of King Henry VIII above the Great Gate of Trinity College is holding a chair leg rather than a sceptre.

Newton's apple

An apple tree by Trinity College's Great Gate is said to be a descendant of the tree from which a falling apple inspired Isaac Newton to formulate the law of gravity.

Speed of sound

It was in the north cloister of Trinity College's Nevile's Court that Newton stamped his foot and timed the echo to calculate the speed of sound.

The Principia

'This most beautiful system of the sun, planets and comets, could only proceed from the counsel and dominion of an intelligent and powerful Being.'

Isaac Newton, *Philosophiae Naturalis Principia Mathematica*, written during his time at Trinity College and published in 1687

Nobel record

Since the beginning of the 20th century, more than 80 Cambridge university members have been awarded Nobel prizes, including over 30 from Trinity College alone.

Literary legends

Lytton Strachey, Leonard Woolf and Thoby Stephen met as undergraduates at Trinity College and in 1899 formed the core of what was to become the Bloomsbury Group, a literary group whose members rejected the taboos and restrictions of the Victorian age.

Remarkably unremarkable

There is a statue of Lord Byron in the Wren Library of Trinity College, even though the poet's undergraduate days here were quite unremarkable. The statue was originally offered to Westminster Abbey but refused on the grounds of Byron's questionable morals.

William and Winnie

Shakespeare's early folios and the original A.A. Milne *Winnie-the-Pooh* manuscript are on display in the library at Trinity College.

Like father, like son

Both A.A. Milne and Christopher Robin of *Winnie-the-Pooh* fame were students at Trinity College.

Royal connections

Prince Charles came up to Trinity College in 1967 and his brother Prince Edward to Jesus College in 1983.

Take a seat

When University Hall (now Clare College) was originally founded in 1326, it is said to have been so poorly funded that it had only two chairs – one for the Master and one for visitors.

Spot the difference

The bridge in the grounds of Clare College dates from 1638 and is the oldest surviving college bridge. A segment missing from one of the 14 stone balls on its parapet is said to represent the designer's revenge for being poorly paid.

Milton's mulberry tree

A mulberry tree in Fellows' Garden is one of the 300 given to Christ's College by James I in 1608. John Milton is said to have written some of his early major poems under this tree.

Round rounds the mulberry tree

The remorseful ghost of a one-time Fellow of Christ's College, Christopher Round, is sometimes seen around the mulberry tree in Fellows' Garden. Apparently responsible for the death of another student, he would pace the garden on endless sleepless nights – a practice carried out until his death 40 years later, and still continued to this day.

Maid, wife and widow

Legend has it that the Countess of Pembroke, founder of Pembroke College, was 'maid, wife and widow' in one day when her husband was killed whilst jousting on their wedding day.

Big brother is watching

Statutes granted to Pembroke College by Edward III included a clause which said members of the college were to spy on their comrades and report them if they drank too much, quarrelled, were extravagant or visited disorderly houses.

Chapel of thanksgiving

In thanksgiving for his release from 18 years imprisoned in the Tower of London, the Bishop of Ely hired his nephew, Christopher Wren, to design Pembroke College Chapel.

Temporary tax

William Pitt the Younger came up to Pembroke College in 1773 aged 14, became Chancellor of the Exchequer at 22 and England's youngest Prime Minister at 24. He will be forever remembered for introducing income tax as a 'temporary measure'.

Child prodigy

St Catharine's College can claim the youngest undergraduate with a boy named William Wotton who came up at the age of nine in the 1600s.

Catharine's wheel

The emblem on the gate to St Catharine's College represents the wheel on which the body of the patron saint of scholars – Catharine of Alexandria – was to have been broken but, miraculously, the wheel shattered at her touch. The Catherine wheel firework is named after her.

Let there be light

Peterhouse was the first college to have electricity, displeasing the laundresses whose washing, laid out on Laundress Green on the banks of the river to dry, was spotted with smuts from the generator.

Fire alarm

Poet Thomas Gray (of 'Elegy Written in a Country Churchyard' fame) was so afraid of fire that he had an iron bar with a rope ladder attached outside his window at Peterhouse. He was frequently the  victim of hoaxers shouting 'Fire!'. The iron bar at his window can still be seen today.

Famous inventors

Peterhouse has produced some of the world's most notable engineers. These include Charles Babbage, who invented the first mechanical computer, Christopher Cockerel, inventor of the hovercraft, and Sir Frank Whittle, inventor of the jet engine. It is thought that Whittle may owe his idea for the jet engine to an exceptionally draughty passage at the college!

Caius's gates

Dr John Caius (pronounced keys) built three gates at Gonville and Caius College to represent the stages of a student's career: he enters at the Gate of Humility

(now leading to the Master's Garden), passes through the Gate of Virtue and leaves through the Gate of Honour. Caius students still pass through the Gate of Honour on their way to receive their degrees.

Making history

Renowned for his work on the Big Bang theory, Stephen Hawking is a Fellow of Gonville and Caius College and Professor of Mathematics – a post once held by Isaac Newton. His book *A Brief History of Time* was on the best-selling list of the *Sunday Times* for more than four years – the longest run for any book in history.

Cambridge Climbers

'Cambridge Climbers' enjoy the challenge of trying to jump Senate House Passage by leaping from the roof of Gonville and Caius College to the Senate House.

American independence

In 1776 three Cambridge graduates –
Thomas Lynch (Gonville and Caius),
Thomas Nelson (Trinity) and Arthur
Middleton (St John's) – were among the
signatories of the American Declaration
of Independence.

Honouring Harvard

John Harvard, founder of Harvard
University, is commemorated in a stained-
glass window in the chapel of Emmanuel
College. He was one of Cambridge's many
graduates who were among New
England's early settlers.

It's a record

Cambridge holds the record for the longest run of wins in University Boat Race history, clocking up 13 successive victories from 1924 to 1936.

A favourite pastime

'… a walk by the waters of the Cam was my favourite way of spending the afternoons.'

Alfred Harry Lawrence, *Reminiscences of Cambridge Life by D.C.*, 1889

JOHN HARVARD   LARCKE CHANGRTON

For or against?

The first recorded motion of Selwyn College's debating society was against 'further operations in the matter of the Channel Tunnel'. This was in 1883.

London Bridge has fallen down

The floor of the main entrance hall in Wolfson College is made from slices of granite from the dismantled London Bridge; the main part of the bridge is now in Arizona, USA.

A Cambridge first

Britain's first women's residential college started in Hitchin in 1869 but was named Girton when, in 1873, it moved to a village of the same name, a safe distance from Cambridge and its men. The women were taught by visiting Cambridge lecturers.

Archaeologist's achievement

The archaeologist Dorothy Garrod, who studied at Newnham College, became the first female professor at Cambridge University in 1939.

A stitch in time

Homerton College – a teacher training college, originally founded in the village of Homerton in Middlesex in 1852 – was unique in admitting both men and women. Women were allowed to achieve a lower pass in mathematics because needlework occupied much of their time!

Women only

Three of the colleges at Cambridge (New Hall, Newnham and Lucy Cavendish) are still women-only establishments, the rest being mixed.

Royal degree

Queen Elizabeth The Queen Mother was the first woman to be awarded a Cambridge degree when she was made an Honorary Doctor of Law in 1948.

Oldest graduate

In 1997 Mrs Molly Maxwell became Cambridge's oldest graduate at 105.

Comedy greats

The Cambridge Footlights is the world-famous troupe whose members have included some of Britain's greatest comedians and actors of the 20th century, including Jimmy Edwards, Peter Cook, John Cleese, Graham Chapman, Eric Idle, Graeme Garden, Bill Oddie, Tim Brooke-Taylor, Griff Rhys Jones, Stephen Fry, Hugh Laurie, Emma Thompson and Tony Slattery.

What month is it?

May Week – a celebration of the end of the final exams – is held in June each year.

General Admissions

General Admissions is the name of the graduation ceremony held in June, in which the new graduates process wearing gowns and hoods to receive their degrees.

Royal warrant

Henry VIII gave the university a royal warrant to start the Cambridge University Press in 1534, to this day one of the oldest and largest academic and educational publishers in the world.

First bookshop

Cambridge University Press Bookshop in Trinity Street is situated on the site of Britain's first bookshop, dating from 1581.

CAMBRIDGE
UNIVERSITY PRESS

BOOKSHOP

Historic robe suppliers

Ede and Ravenscroft of Trumpington Street, suppliers of academic robes since the 17th century, has made all of England's sovereigns' coronation robes since the time of William III.

Fitzbillies' famous buns

Fitzbillies of Trumpington Street, master bakers for more than three-quarters of a century, are world-famous for their delicious Chelsea buns – so popular that annual subscriptions for a monthly supply delivered by post are available.

Hobson's choice

Hobson's Conduit, the elaborate fountain in Trumpington Street, is named after Thomas Hobson who in 1610 financed the scheme to bring spring water to the city. Hobson was renowned for insisting customers at his livery stables only hired his horses in strict rotation – hence the saying 'Hobson's choice', meaning no choice at all.

Pilots' lights

The Eagle pub in Bene't Street is a restored 17th-century coaching inn. On the ceiling of its Air Force Bar, burnt on with cigarette lighters during the Second World War, are the names and numbers of RAF and US pilots who drank here.

Tall, dark stranger

The ghost of a tall, dark man dressed in a long cloak is said to haunt Michel's bar and brasserie in Northampton Street. Once known as the Oyster Tavern, parts of the building date back more than 500 years.

On your bike

Bicycles are a serious form of transport in
Cambridge, especially as most students at
the University of Cambridge are forbidden
to bring cars.

City dwellers

Cows are still grazed in green open spaces in the centre of Cambridge.

Come to the fair

Cambridge's Strawberry Fair – one of the country's largest festivals of music, entertainment, arts and crafts – has been held for more than 30 years in late spring on Midsummer Common. The Midsummer Fair, held each June, dates back to the Middle Ages.

Fair inspiration

A leper hospital in a village near Cambridge was granted the right to hold a fair by King John in 1211, which developed into the famous Stourbridge Fair. By the 17th century it was reputedly 'not only the greatest in the whole nation, but in the world' and was worthy of comment by a number of writers including John Bunyan who modelled Vanity Fair in *Pilgrim's Progress* on it, which in turn prompted Thackeray's *Vanity Fair*. But by the mid 18th century Stourbridge Fair had passed its peak and was finally abolished in 1933.

The bumps

'Bumps' is a rowing event held on the narrow River Cam at Lent and in June in which the eights start one behind the other, 1½ lengths apart, and aim to bump the boat in front, thus replacing it in the next day's race.

The Backs

The area of lawns and meadows along the
Cam known as the Backs is so-named
because this is where many of the oldest
colleges back on to the river.

Lord's lines

I past beside the reverend walls
In which of old I wore the gown ...
And caught once more the distant shout,
The measured pulse of racing oars
Among the willows ...

From *In Memoriam A.H.H.*, 1850,
by Alfred, Lord Tennyson, who
attended Trinity College

Cambridge blue

Athletes who represent the university in such major sports as rugby, cricket or the boat race are awarded a 'full blue', which entitles them to wear a pale blue blazer.

Blazing jackets

The term 'blazer' comes from the scarlet jackets worn by oarsmen from the Lady Margaret Boat Club. Founded in 1825, it is the oldest college club on the Cam.

Club's challenge

Members of Cambridge's Lady Margaret Boat Club challenged Oxford to a boat race in 1829 and so began the University Boat Race.

First boat race

The first University Boat Race took place at Henley-on-Thames on 10 June 1829. Subsequent races were rowed from Westminster to Putney until the race moved upstream in 1845, since which time the famous Putney to Mortlake course has been used.

Practice makes perfect

The Cambridge crew of the Oxford v. Cambridge boat race practises on the Great Ouse at Ely, where river conditions closely match those of the Thames.